Little Book of Special Thoughts

Fizzy Moon®

...with love x

This edition published by Ravette Publishing 2011.

ISBN: 978-1-84161-354-3

RAVETTE PUBLISHING

You have a
very special
place in my
heart

I can't imagine what
I'd do without a special
friend like you

A hug
is a great gift -
One size fits all

It doesn't matter
where you are, I know you're
right here in my heart

You fill my world
with sunshine

If balloons were wishes
about to come true
I'd pick out the biggest and
best for you

Too much of a
good thing is
wonderful!

Some people make
the world more special -
Just by being in it

A nice thought just
occurred to me... You!

May today
be the kind of day
you had in mind

When I count my
blessings I always
count you twice

Learn from yesterday,

Live for today,

Hope for tomorrow

Life is not measured by the
number of breaths we take
but by the Moments that
take our breath away!

A cup of tea,
a laugh or two-
happy moments
shared with you

Be yourself -
everyone else is taken!

Everything is twice
as nice when shared

You are my sunshine

The seat next to me is reserved for life

Other Fizzy Moon titles available...

	ISBN	Price
Little Book of Love	978-1-84161-353-6	£4.99

HOW TO ORDER Please send a cheque/postal order in £ sterling, made payable to 'Ravette Publishing' for the cover price of books and allow the following for post & packaging...

UK & BFPO   70p for the first book & 40p per book thereafter
Europe and Eire   £1.30 for the first book & 70p per book thereafter
Rest of the world   £2.20 for the first book & £1.10 per book thereafter

RAVETTE PUBLISHING LTD
PO Box 876, Horsham, West Sussex RH12 9GH
Tel: 01403 711443 Fax: 01403 711554 Email: ravettepub@aol.com

Prices and availability are subject to change without prior notice.